KAREN KELLOCK
FRENEMY
LIAR

FRENEMY LIAR

RED NEW DEAL

Karen Kellock Ph.D.

Manual for
Superior Men

This is a complete theory based on Einstein physics,
Political Psychology, Systems Theory
and Archetypal Psychiatry.

FORMULA

All success attraction
All disease obstruction
All recovery elimination

You must fast on all three

OBSTRUCTIONS:

People
Habit
Food

FRENEMY LIAR

You're a genius and it's obvious and they're dumb as rats but copious. Lock the gate to be free of whatever's happening outside--now every day is great. People did nothing but hold you back and trip you up so now just look UP! Many grow up with rejection, no one wanted em. Everyone wants something so be shrewd to prevent a disaster happening. Wild animals are nocturnal to avoid humans and I've done that too to be a good student.

FRIENDS WRECK DESTINY

COVETING WHAT YOU HAVE
SAINTS LOVE BEING ALONE
MEDIOCRE OR MAGNIFICENT?
REGARD YOUR DIFFERENCES
THE WAY YOU BOUNCED BACK
THE CHOSEN ARE TESTED WITH WORSE
FRENEMIES RUN IN CROWDS
THESE ROADS YOU TRAVEL ALONE
10,000 FALL BY YOUR SIDE
MARVELS WHEN ALONE
DISTRACTIONS AND GOOD INTENTIONS
FRIENDS CAN'T SEE YOUR VISION
FRIENDS SPEAK FEARS
THEY DON'T HAVE YOUR BACK
NEW FRIENDS, NEW BOUNDARIES
NO COMPROMISE OR RECIPROCITY
THEY THINK YOU NEED THEM

FRIENDS WRECK DESTINY

COVETING WHAT YOU HAVE

I hate to burst your bubble about people but if you gotta money bag they're gonna be wanting that.

I settle things in my dreams, like right and wrong: Like is it ok to change a recipe then pass it on?

Whenever you have cringy memories, count your blessings. You're in a mansion & they're not see.

We are most powerful when alone, when there's no one distracting us or pulling our energy down.

Avoidance: she was always suggesting things when I've been alone so much you can't tell me anything.

When with others it feels like pure chaos! When alone I'm totally engrossed in an inner world so nice.

SAINTS LOVE BEING ALONE

I love being alone. After hitting bottom & rising to the top anything else is chaos and I wanna go home!

Start speaking up for what you deserve--what you've EARNED! Your comeback is historical girl.

Even though it fell in my lap I EARNED what I have cuz God gave it to me after all I endured way back.

THEY weren't blessed but they want your bounty. That isn't how it works honey so stay away phony.

FRIENDS WRECK DESTINY

God said "double for your trouble" so He paid me back after all that. You deserve it all, that's a fact.

Not only did He give it He'll allow you to KEEP it, which is hard in these days when others are losing it.

You must realize what you really worked hard for. What you saw as a failure God tallied up the hours.

MEDIOCRE OR MAGNIFICENT?

What you saw as mediocre compared to others God saw as magnificent for your faith & the hours.

You're a powerhouse cuz you did all that ALONE. They coulda never done that so they stay below.

I learned to not fear evil while in the shadow of death, to be totally alone in the desert and LOVED it.

They could NEVER be alone. They gotta be surrounded by people or forever answering the dam phone.

They are GROUPIES man, face it. They are totally different from you, a chosen and loving it.

Take a good look at your family & friends. They always have someone around or on the phone, amen?

When I got away I still felt encroached on night and day. They weren't here but I still felt that way.

That's because we're DIFFERENT and that must be realized so feelings of encroachment subside.

REGARD YOUR DIFFERENCES

When you see how very different you are you'll feel deserving of all you have without feeling so bad.

FRIENDS WRECK DESTINY

Those people are weak minded though they self-congratulate like they know all about it.

Their whole life is cluttered with all kinds of stress & confusion. Clear mindedness is rare son.

They would "die" to be in your position right now but are unwilling to do the work to be a know how.

You went thru the storm ALONE while they panicked and stayed down with people all around.

For all your went thru the blessings coming to you are endless. Be separate for they don't deserve this.

THE WAY YOU BOUNCED BACK

The way you bounced back from rock bottom to mountain top ALONE is why your star shone.

The best feeling in the world is knowing you did it alone and your way. You healed your own wounds ok.

There were so many obstacles coming against you but you fought these battles with only God too.

We fought these generational curses by ourselves. Being chosen we got the worse attacks, ouch!

We had to go thru poverty, homelessness, sickness or just having to beg rides or kiss up: STRESS.

THE CHOSEN ARE TESTED WITH WORSE

We had to go thru these things worse, because being chosen they were TESTS making us the best.

After going thru that fiery furnace alone now we're getting ready to COME OUT like pure gold.

FRIENDS WRECK DESTINY

You will never doubt yourself again after realizing what you went through ALONE in the lion's den.

They're scared. They have no power or anointing like you do chosen one and they aren't that rare.

They thought after sacrificing you and selling you out you'd be done for but you shot right back up!

What they did with their bad behavior is send you back to God. You repented of your sins, unflawed.

FRENEMIES RUN IN CROWDS

Don't forget so-called friends. Every time you look up their moving in packs/roaming in crowds, amen?

What about your narcissistic ex. How he let people in and put you down for being alone, a reject!

Every time they see you you're by yourself. You know how strong you gotta be to be a lone elf?

You gotta be so strong to eat by yourself, go to the gym by yourself: it gave you strength/great wealth.

You fell down but kept pressing toward the mark. You showed great resilience right from the start.

You fought for your life, prosperity, discovery and generational wealth. So you stayed by yourself.

THESE ROADS YOU TRAVEL ALONE

Some roads you must travel by yourself: no friends, relationship nor partner, but it means wealth.

It was just me and God and I was ok with that cuz that's when I got the most blessings, totally awed.

FRIENDS WRECK DESTINY

Every time I was by myself He gave me a new level of anointing, feeling strong, optimistic & loving.

Every time I was alone God sent me more protective angels making me strong, warm and aglow.

Think about it: those talking against you are always hanging out in crowds: busybodies full of it!

Think about it: people who lied on you are always hanging with other people. Officious twits!

Those who could never surpass you are constantly teaming with others to put you down Sue.

10,000 FALL BY YOUR SIDE

While alone 10,000 can fall at your side but you're protected. Secret competitions are discredited.

Those dumb others can never surpass you because you have no constant distractions like they do.

These are all the advantages you'll have walking alone. It's such a trip sharing life with God, aglow!

Think about it: you finally have no one stressing you out & they leave you're no longer pissed off.

Friends putting their "good times" up on facebook aren't putting up their bad times when forsook!

Not having any friends allows us to refocus back onto God. People distract and all are flawed.

It may be a dopamine rush when they wanna do something but it distracts from destiny.

Fast on friends for awhile and you will see: an inner world is triggered that is so fancy and free!

FRIENDS WRECK DESTINY

It seems like they all want something, "friends" now is transactional. I got sick of all of it em all.

When alone I'm so hyper-efficient and clever. When interrupted with "friendship" this is all over.

MARVELS WHEN ALONE

When alone: I bought new speakers, the absolute best, after tedious researching for days all the rest.

When friend-fasting, God takes me on a proprioceptive journey from which there's no return: destiny!

What do I need friends for, they just wanna change my plans. They're just a dam encumbrance man.

Our judgements are always clouded due to distractions. This is not freedom: question all decisions.

Being chosen, you don't need anyone but God. With friends you're insecure like you need the flawed.

"Friends" are constantly sowing seeds of doubt. You sure you wanna go there? You know it all.

You get an unusual hunch & it's brilliant. Then you talk to a friend about it and suddenly question it.

DISTRACTIONS AND GOOD INTENTIONS

All distractions are couched as "good intentions". That's the road to hell ya' know and it's not God son.

They get worried you're too isolated then come to the gate and it's locked. They tell another, yuk!

Friends are naturally officious and distort your life. You don't need another mind, it's always strife.

FRIENDS WRECK DESTINY

Friends interfere in decisions you make. Their "good intentions" warp God's unique hunches, ok?

They "only wanna help" and that may be true, but believe me you're encumbered by the crew.

Friends are constantly putting things in your ear that are negative or doubtful and I'm had my full.

Just as officious are extended family. It drove me crazy when that sister in law was always meddling.

FRIENDS CAN'T SEE YOUR VISION

Friends don't see the vision that you have. God put it in YOU not others without your nature: FACT.

Meddling, gossiping, good intention officious interrupting: I felt encroached upon constantly.

The more I withdrew the more compelled they were to encroach too. It's a natural human reaction Sue.

They were like spurned ex-lovers compelled to come around closer: I felt encroached on forever!

They get with your other friends and they advise each other on how to react to your isolation sister.

They project fears onto your vision since it doesn't apply to them. They're too weak, thus their reaction.

FRIENDS SPEAK FEARS

Friends speak fears out loud and you take it in: now it's your reality. There goes your magic destiny.

Sowing seeds of doubt, guilt, shame or social fears: that's how it was when close to the dears.

FRIENDS WRECK DESTINY

Friend-fasting teaches how to enjoy our own company and advocate for ourselves as magic elves.

Friends feel they're giving more than they are and ask for favors in return. It becomes outrageous, grrrr!

Waiting for a friend to stick up for me is futile: I must learn to advocate for myself which I do now.

Waiting for others to back you up is always frustrating. They don't have the guts nor knowledge honey.

THEY DON'T HAVE YOUR BACK

When they don't have your back you feel discouraged, frustrated & disappointed. This is imprisonment!

I began to feel I was unworthy of being stuck up for. They just don't have the right perspective sir.

I enjoy my own company so much that no one can compete. They're always just a nuisance see.

The worst part is if you get a windfall they expect part of it. Just for being friends? It's pure bullshit.

Setting boundaries: Not have friends allows you to see what you'll tolerate and what you won't see.

With friends around your true boundaries become blurred cuz you go in denial about the herd.

NEW FRIENDS, NEW BOUNDARIES

If you make new friends you can establish boundaries early on. A brand new respect is gained hon'.

I'm not showing up for you, I'm not going to jail for you, I've got kids. Don't bother me anymore sis!

FRIENDS WRECK DESTINY

Friendship implies **COMPROMISE** and it's a dirty word in the life of a chosen which I totally despise.

They do something for you and it's like you're indebted forever. Now you gotta change plans: bummer.

While friend-fasting you don't have to explain, justify or rationalize. I can move freely free of you guys.

NO COMPROMISE OR RECIPROCITY

Compromise and reciprocity are pure encumbrance when it comes to the destiny of chosen see.

As soon as they're in they presume on friendship for this and that. Like borrowing money, the brats.

Worse, friends wanna borrow things. They see something they want, that's always how it is see.

Changing your plans, instilling doubt and expecting favors: I've had it with "friends" up to here!

As soon as they got a foot in they gossip and betray all your secrets man so watch what you tell em.

Having a friend is like having a spy in the house. They're more trouble than they're worth, I promise.

Who else can spill the goods [gossip, a leak in the house] than someone who's gotten close?

THEY THINK YOU NEED THEM

They act like you need them, what an insult! It's always the dunning-kruger effect with these nuts.

Learning these principals about people is the greatest road to glory. It'll save your very life, truly.

FRIENDS WRECK DESTINY

The crap I had to go thru to learn em is more than you could ever fathom so listen/learn your lesson.

They get a step in and learn all your secrets friend. They're a trojan horse till the war ends.

Just letting her in one bit caused me to go nuts, have fits and be up all night trying to figure it out.

Not only this, they involve you in THEIR business. You start to give advice & here we go again sis.

Then they want you to meet their friends. They discuss you behind the scenes then flip the script see.

ENERGY THIEVES

FEEL THE FICKLE
IDEALIZATION-DISCARD: HARD ROAD
VICTIMS OF NARCISSISTS
MARK OF A QUEEN: ESCAPE THIS SCENE
KNOWLEDGE IS THE SOLUTION
CORDIAL BUT DISTANT
EMPATH SYSTEM WITH NARCISSIST
RUTHLESS APATHY AFTER LOVING
ILLUSIONS OF PERFECT UNION
HE SIGNALS DOMINANCE, SHE LOVES IT
PRIDE IS SELF-AGGRANDIZEMENT
HE'S NOT THE PRIZE HE'S WRAPPED IN
EASILY OPENED ATTACHMENT SYSTEMS
EMPATHIC OVERSTEPPING OF BOUNDARIES
ENERGY ROBBING
PHYSICAL RAMIFICATIONS
SYMPATHETIC DOMINANCE: WEARING OUT
POOR HEALTH INCREASES DEVALUATION

ENERGY THIEVES:
CHEMISTRY, ATTACHMENT AND ENERGY EXCHANGE SYSTEMS

FEEL THE FICKLE

He tried to inferiorize/break you to control you but now you're gone forever having seen the ol' goat.

Fickle people will change suddenly. Careful of your broken heart when around the unhealthy.

It's a miserable existence to be addicted to people since more times than not they disappoint you.

Only the strong can separate themselves without loss of identity in any way: God is enough ok.

As a son/daughter of God you must never force yourself on nonfriends, being on the begging end.

Healing cannot begin until you allow distance. While engaged with cold people you feel the fickle.

People constantly rejecting and breaking you prevent healing too. Get distance to be renewed.

IDEALIZATION-DISCARD: HARD ROAD

Idealization phase: they're good at putting people on a pedestal but soon after pushing them off.

Narcissists are very easily disappointed in people and will devalue them in a minute too.

They idealize you, they deflate you: a human zoo with one who strikes without warning too.

ENERGY THIEVES

They're mad their fantasies weren't fulfilled, that you let em down, their inner emptiness revealed.

Devaluation occurs [cold shoulder, humiliation, destroy reputation] when infantile rage is triggered.

Like an infant with new toy suddenly smashing it: you didn't meet my needs tho' I can't explain it.

It's not as pretty as I thought. It's become boring so I'll discard it: that's the uncertainty she's got.

The interpersonal carnage the narcissist leaves thru the years does incalculable damage/tears.

He's enamored with new kid on the block--the rising genius--but soon discards him as irrelevance.

Romantically or professionally they leave a trail of disaster emotionally and won't change see.

Viewing others as extensions of themselves: he sees others by how they make HIM feel that's all.

If you're nice & shiny it mirrors themselves but if weak the mirror's cracked and they discard/rebel.

VICTIMS OF NARCISSISTS

Until you disengage you'll be sad, happy, heartbroken, delusional, ecstatic, confused: MAD.

The lovebombing/idealization phase is short-lived as the narcissist becomes deeply disappointed.

Devaluation begins subtly: failing to show up, disinterest, silence, comparing/triangulating.

All these signal the empath's strong inner critic and that's where she's triggered/addicted.

ENERGY THIEVES

During lovebombing the empath's inner critic is put to bed/greatly reduced but then he discards.

An empath's core values--hyperactive attachment, need to please, inner critic--makes her victim.

Due to core values the devaluation throws the empath into downward spiral of confusion/despair.

It's a confused, disorientating and painful sense of paradise lost: the feelings after the loveblast.

Having felt loved, adored, appreciated by narcissist she now feels crushed by her defectiveness.

Tho' subtle the empath's need to please, attachment and critic are massively triggered see.

Her lived experience of a fantasy--not abstract--makes her want it back and that's her new map.

And thus a user--not a lover--can extract material gains from empaths by whetting this hunger.

Learning these signs is the way out: then never let em know what you know--transcend, be above.

MARK OF A QUEEN: ESCAPE THIS SCENE

The mark of a queen is how soon she'll cut you loose without thought or a cringe, now vamoose.

From the high of being totally perfect & loved to the low of being totally worthless & dumped.

With soul tie deactivation she feels so much lighter getting every drawer in her home in order.

With his depedestalization--decapitation, a fizzled out illusion--she instantly expands, oh man!

ENERGY THIEVES

With soul tie deactivation you'll be skipping around like a madwoman--mad with relief after bedlam.

Show the world why your way is best. Prove it: "Does it work" is a discovery's most important test.

KNOWLEDGE IS THE SOLUTION

The narcissist's devices lose power the minute you learn about em and so does he after knowing him.

You don't see their neurosis until they have authority over you, then it frustrates/feeling helpless.

Living on main drag without a fence was like being in a prison surrounded by thugs/a sitting duck.

Solution is to be aware of your attachment and energy exchange systems--and to insulate em.

As you become self-aware you also hear his intentional trigger words and finally, you turn.

God doesn't want you in this dark space anymore. Of fear, guilt, soul ties and rejections galore.

An energy vampire feeding off of you and you're the host: the one frantic, unhappy, rundown.

In other words, we gentle ones are slaves and targets until we build our boundaries/man up.

Mature, or be the recipient of their deepest and meanest projections with great embarrassment.

The energy flow of empath to narcissist is continuous while post inception he couldn't care less.

Having resolved lower rungs like ridicule now we move on to higher discoveries/talents so cool.

ENERGY THIEVES

The key to success is to self-forgive or you'll be stuck in remorse: savior archetype starts as an ass.

Being interested in the narcissist [have they moved on, are they thinking of me] robs further energy.

STOP IT: It is pathological to be detail-obsessed with the narcissist for it further robs energy sis.

CORDIAL BUT DISTANT

Have cordial but distant relations or you'll go down a rabbit hole of unnecessary complications.

We lose ourselves thru enmeshment where we don't need to be. For queens independence is key.

After a period of unnecessary enmeshment--sucked in--a new vista opens up and we say "never again".

Masculine energy is not gaming/breaking a woman but watching over her--get that straight ladies.

Once she sees triangulation as part of the discard phase [it hurts equally guys] it's easier, aye.

EMPATH SYSTEM WITH NARCISSIST

The poor empath in love with a narcissist means heartbreak rode like he intends to do this.

Any love interest of a narcissist is an infantile expression of his idealization seen as "love".

The empath's core wounds [feeling fundamentally unworthy] are retriggered and now he hates her.

Now she's incapable of getting back to the lovely idealization phase: now she really pays.

ENERGY THIEVES

At this point the narcissist unleashes his hostility and rage towards the empath: she goes mad.

She fails as the idealized partner **THEY** had imagined them to be: royal couple no more you see.

Being such a chameleon she takes this all on as an archetype of rejection, sin and scorn.

RUTHLESS APATHY AFTER LOVING

This is the narcissist archetypically manifesting the tyrant by being now ruthlessly apathetic.

The tyrant king banishes people who've not met his standards, to mirror him, so he beheads.

Why? To take revenge on empath, unleash rage that they weren't the perfect partner they thought.

They may continue the relationship for supply: watching the frantic attempts in the other's cries.

The empath will do anything to reestablish relation so is used for her time, money, body or as secretary.

Drip-feeding her a diet of intermittent reinforcement keeps her a lapdog broken queen lunatic.

Push-pull: the empath is idealized, it's withdrawn leaving her in cycle of confusion and fear, aye.

All narcissists use intermittent reinforcement of rewards and punishments which hook the empath.

He's a huge buzz word to her. Solution: unhook and understand, you'll see him as a cartoon soon.

In the short honeymoon phase the empath's attachment system is activated/she feels needed.

ENERGY THIEVES

A spike in love chemicals, hormones and neurotransmitters precedes a crash soon after.

The crushing sense of defeat comes with biologically hardwired attachment systems see.

It's **NEVER** how he feels today, it's how he feels tomorrow and the next day: consistency.

ILLUSIONS OF PERFECT UNION

During discard the illusion of perfect union is shattered for example by his flaunting a new partner.

With the narcissist it's pervasive, he takes revenge and he humiliates even ruins her at the end.

His rage and vindictiveness shows a deep need to destroy and strip the other of dignity.

Smear campaigns, stalking, threats of intimidation are sure to happen with the end of the union.

Narcissists essentially wish to destroy the other, hurting her is not enough and he can be quite clever.

Almost always, the narcissistic relationship after the idealization phase turns destructive.

Relationships never work due to his structure of all good or all bad, all beautiful or worthless to have.

For him relationship is a self-enhancement strategy to bolster grandiosity-- they're an extension see.

His hot appraisal of his partner is short and rapidly fades: the perfection illusion is shattered ok.

The narcissist has great success initiating relationships but never healthy long-term lasting links.

ENERGY THIEVES

Grandiose narcissists succeed in sexual encounters and relationship initiation but that's it son.

Grandiose narcissists have greater sexual access in the relationship market place, now why is this?

At first they seem desirable/attractive as potential mates, putting empath in a hypnotic trance.

HE SIGNALS DOMINANCE, SHE LOVES IT

The bright traits signaling confidence and dominance: for approval they self-market themselves.

They adapt to the environment presenting themselves in the most promising light: they approach "Hi"!

They don't have inhibitions or fears of rejection, they can approach without any deliberation.

Without fear of criticism they're motivated by the rewards of sex, supply, money, admiration.

The narcissist is unmoved by banishment, disapproval, ridicule so seems more dominant and cool.

Lower levels of anxiety/neuroticism when meeting a potential mate gives them social power ok.

With low anxiety he's able to move far more energy out to the other person, magnifying his charisma.

They maintain the illusion of confident independence but for approval they're deeply dependent.

Because they're insensitive to social censure they have more dominance for sexual appeal/allure.

Pride: the core emotion making the empath vulnerable thinking she can change him/she is able.

ENERGY THIEVES

Pride's a form of self-deception or bloated self-importance to uplift, forgive and transform.

PRIDE IS SELF-AGGRANDIZEMENT

Pride makes her think she can change a self-absorbed, arrogant and destructive personality.

The sweet gentle but prideful empath envisions him changing into someone caring and genuine.

Blinding delusion: her great capacity for love will transform his arrogance to devoted allegiance.

Pride is self-deception and an exaggerated self-importance coming back to hurt her and fast.

As a major blind spot it's destructive if she's unaware of it as she usually always is: love is blind sis.

Her destructive pride sucks her into the orbit of the narcissist and there she sticks, sad/sick.

Pride makes them keep on giving of themselves tirelessly along with resources to this guy.

Pride is a defense against shame and for the empath it comes from feeling unworthy in early days.

The solution to pride is it's opposite, humility: knowing you can't do anything about it see.

Pride is one of the seven deadly sins but humility is a universally recognized virtue see.

Humility acknowledges the empath's limitations: that love does not conquer all/her power is nil.

Pride invades the boundaries of others. Overstepping ruins relationships quick, they feel smothered.

ENERGY THIEVES

Underlying issues lock empaths up. We all must confront lies we tell ourselves, this is growing up.

The empath becomes a pathological giver in response to this set up of him dominating or rejecting her.

Covert contracts are unwritten rules operating when she's giving: her assuming he'll give in.

HE'S NOT THE PRIZE HE'S WRAPPED IN

He's not the prize he's wrapped as. Initially captivating with time the contradictions overwhelm us.

Narcissists have "low neuroticism": indifferent to social banishment they just forge ahead.

The empath's willingness to self-sacrifice makes them the ultimate prey for the narcissist.

The empath's delusion is to give-give-give assuming reciprocity but that never comes see.

A narcissist is incapable of feeling her pain--there is no give and take--but her resentment is delayed.

It's an attachment & energy-exchange system: forming TIES is a neurobiological compulsion.

Being totally dependent we form a bond [hopefully] with our primary caregivers: TRAUMA, early.

These bonds are also psychospiritual: forming links with something greater than the self/the ALL.

EASILY OPENED ATTACHMENT SYSTEMS

What is chemistry/empathy? An activated attachment system also controls ENERGY flow see.

ENERGY THIEVES

Activated attachment systems allow free flow of energy between two people, a potential evil.

The mother-infant tie is pre-verbal via eye contact etc. Call this chemistry or a transcendent charisma.

This system activates portals in the mother to send and receive energy from her infant, the other.

Empaths for various reasons have easily activated attachment systems and here's the problem.

Her energy system [opening to others] is easily switched ON: make note of this daughter/watch out.

The positive side for empaths is developing bonds with others but the negative side is: psychosis.

Forming bonds with those who don't want her, couldn't care less and are running the other way.

EMPATHIC OVERSTEPPING OF BOUNDARIES

It sets up the empath to overstep boundaries and assume way too much ["let's do lunch"].

This sets them up for nonreciprocal relationships and resentments of a weird outsider looking in.

Compared to the empath the attachment system of the narcissist is totally dysfunctional, read on:

Attachment systems are based on the capacity to form enduring bonds to different/higher beings.

Attachment systems: difficult for the narcissist who habitually views others as extensions of self.

He lacks the needed coherent sense of self to "attach" to anything, to see the other as the "other".

ENERGY THIEVES

Her attachment system is activated, he shuts her down until the next time she opens to a mate.

It wasn't so much "emotional immaturity" as it was an activated and open attachment system.

The thing to do after a mistake like that is to act like it never happened: they assumed wrong facts.

Hence, the energetic flow with a narcissist is only one way despite initial devices to open you up ok.

A narcissist knows how to extract sympathy or sexual energy, that's what he does to everybody.

ENERGY ROBBING

At first the narcissist is feeding off the energy of the empath, AKA energy-robbing/vampirism.

This makes the empath, tuned to the needs of others, far more vulnerable as prey to the wolf.

VICTIMS: vastly active/highly porous energy fields with easily activated attachment systems.

The empath's attachment system is chronically activated by the painful devices of the narcissist.

Put all memory in a bag and throw the bag out. Don't go thru any part--water under the bridge now.

The empath enters into a distractive parasitic relationship with what is an energy sponge.

The narcissist is locked into the parasitic relationship where energy's stolen from the empath.

A narcissist thrives on energy of others compensating inner emptiness so at times create trouble sis.

ENERGY THIEVES

Creative rivalries, making comparisons, triggering with words or ghosting are devices or all of em.

Solution is to be aware of your attachment and energy exchange systems--and to insulate em.

As you become self-aware you also hear his intentional trigger words and finally, you turn.

God doesn't want you in this dark space anymore. Of fear, guilt, soul ties and rejections galore.

An energy vampire feeding off of you and you're the host: the one frantic, unhappy, rundown.

Empaths: be aware of this dynamic with attachment and energy systems and insulate them.

End work: Mind boundaries, keep pride in check, learn assertion/to say NO, be authentic/bold.

PHYSICAL RAMIFICATIONS

I was never so traumatized as when after I changed it was my own family I didn't recognize.

Stress is psychological but perpetual instability/anxiety leaves a physical impact upon the body.

Stress of continuous uncertainty with reversals between idealization and minimization with gaslighting.

Interpersonal stress is the greatest pain of all: divorce, death, bullies or nonreciprocal relationships.

Don't fear the past, it was a lower rung and necessary for your bright future to last, no remorse lass.

It is interpersonal stress people seek psychologists for and it's even worse than physical stressors.

ENERGY THIEVES

This system locks the empath into chronic inflammation due to uncertainty and lack of equilibrium.

Narcissist: a parasite extracting maximal energy from the partner whose health fails thereafter.

SYMPATHETIC DOMINANCE: WEARING OUT

Sympathetic dominance: Fight/Flight, dealing with stress, activation mode are predominant.

Blood pressure and overall increased inflammation all because of who she loves/believes in.

Chronically activated sympathetic dominance comes from the necessity of her eternal vigilance.

Bamboozled by the narcissist's push-pull behaviors, over-concern over what he does all over.

Chronic stress produces inflammatory molecules with bad effects on every organ in the body too.

On the brain the constant stress creates neurological disorders like chronic fatigue syndrome.

Increased inflammatory response sets the stage for inflammatory disease in all systems see.

The second physical mark is slowed metabolism, esp. middle aged female empaths feeling ageism.

The body slows down the metabolic rate as an adaptive mechanism to deal with stress or hate.

Brain fog and fatigue are least of these responses, most become embedded to death or hospice.

She gaining weight and can't lose it under the pressure of the chronic stress and that nails it.

Frenemy Liar

The more you shield yourself from reality the more you invite predation.

Lock the gate to be free of whatever's happening outside the gate--now *every* day is great.

You're a genius and it's obvious, they're dumb as rats but copious, we're falling into a vortex.

People did nothing but hold you back and trip you up so it's just God we gotta please, look UP!

It never shoulda happened ever but really, you didn't know any better.

Many grow up with rejection, no one wanted em.

To be a writer gotta go thru the ringer first: squashed and burned then of humans you've learned.

Everyone wants something and you gotta be shrewd to save yourself from a disaster happening.

Wild animals have become nocturnal to avoid humans and I've done that too to be a good student.

The wicked never question what they want to do, the righteous are restrained/humble too.

FRENEMY LIAR

It hurts being a majority of one and it's lonely at the top but you must before you turn to dust.

Closer you get to just your own life--free of interruptions--the happier you'll be/no strife.

Since 1970 the American IQ has decreased four points from immigration, trauma and dying out.

Without self-knowledge of importance of personal boundaries my early life was one big trauma.

All you do is complain about people when all you have to do is lock the gate and block out evil.

Appeared at their cabin door with a shotgun: the proper stance when you can't trust anyone.

With sickness the household becomes ingrown and that is best because we're making gold.

Even the news isn't as interesting as your own mind so get offa that thing and muse, think, dream.

You're gonna make it cuz you're for the Highest.

You're not alone/forsaken but under God's wing, hidden.

Around the superior man everything comes into perfect order.

Other people judge, I size people up.

It is not Christian to accept their wrongdoing.

FRENEMY LIAR

I'd rather you not talk than say nothing.

Facebook is censuring me so I'm done,but there's plenty to read here, hon'

They've been raised in postmodernism. They don't argue, they censure. Goodbye to my Facebook Era.

Herd works off mutual energy like a flock of birds assuming the flight pattern is correct, surely.

He may be cute but open his mouth and it's not astute but mediocre: redundancy in poser's suit.

Facebook/Youtube bans Infowars but keeps Antifa and Farrikan. Clear prejudice, unequal weights man.

Instead of repeating in your head "why" does he do things just see him as a budding criminal.

God gave me a fresh start--off the charts--and my past sins didn't leave a trace, He had em erased.

When I take the day off, creativity takes off--relaxation from work tension brings on creative action.

Have office hours and if you sit there and do nothing, *more power*.

Since internet is infinite I get hooked on tangents then mentally absorbed for weeks lovin' it.

Don't expect em to understand you, just be nice. If you're managing the herd it's not a fight.

"These people are insufferable" means kids/pets have to suffer em.

FRENEMY LIAR

Satan and his children love to attack you personally since they lack God's true authority.

All who sin are slaves.

At first they really have it but then due to immorality lose it.

Creativity is a funny thing. It's brittle, oversensitive, can't be forced, vulnerable so get away I say.

I just must have total solitude--SOLO--to develop on my own accord as God designed/bestowed.

Altho' it should be the opposite, the traumatized melt down and let em in, increasing the illness/sin.

Traumatized lose boundaries then the problem floods in creating insanity. Lesson: stay calm always.

Porn addiction: need it more but enjoy it less. Thrills you one day but doesn't do it the next.

Even your own family hates your guts/reject you for being right. Good's called evil, overnight.

Grandstand: Using her personal tragedy to become famous and rich (spot light on the witch).

Though they'll deny/ban/block truth it starts to work on em and they lose power/creative juice.

As it starts to work on em (truth vs. dogma) they'll start to bloat and beautiful planes are lost.

What you have is years of experience and no one can argue with that so don't compare/never covet.

FRENEMY LIAR

Just cuz the past was bad doesn't mean the future will be. Life is in stages while God is forming thee.

When they want you to adapt your work to their limitations--forget that, go solo and transcend em.

Once you know how fast things turn you are humble and unassuming and that starts your winning.

In an instant you can lose it all. Knowing that--living on the razor's edge--is what keeps you on top.

Don't wear the bruised past but open up to blissful future for if you carry it along you're dead sister.

Forgive past actors teaching you boundaries and solitude--they were spooks but it's what it took.

Forgive yourself, it was the influence of other people. You were just too weak and in came evil.

Forgive yourself it was a demon and you were too weak to control him.

What I've learned in life is people aren't nice.

You're gross in your approach and we'll never be in touch so good luck, rot.

It helps so much to know it was a demon cuz then there's no need for explainin' just forget him.

Hysteria is tied to *dependence*.

They're either family or not. We're down to basics and God said our enemies are in the house.

FRENEMY LIAR

Sin destroys decades of your life and if He's given you up to it you'll have no control/filled with strife.

Treating children like permanent victims is a bad idea but the politically correct were taught that way.

To skillfully manage human relations you must first know about em and that's my reason for livin'.

It wasn't rejection they just reacted to your sin archetype then life filled in/they became busy overnight.

If you preachers don't mention sin let alone hell, how will they know/why would they repent y'all?

Those who think it's a predestined groove: work all day. Those who see it as free will: nothing to say.

I'm driven every moment by the (divine predestined) groove which gives me most fulfillment.

Have faith in your inspired work though it doesn't sell. It's just a test and only the future can tell.

The more important word: "No". The most important wisdom: People are not nice ya' know.

Joel Osteen is a "pagan religionist/quasi pantheist"--see, there are words for Christian vs. new agers.

A watered down gospel is no gospel at all. It's but a cheap sickening thing of no use to y'all.

More resistance = less motion in your life.

FRENEMY LIAR

Repentance is the key unlocking your predestined groove. Stay in sin and there's no breakthrough.

Repent = fall into your groove. Stay in sin = remain a clerk, gopher, stooge.

Get the dogs and kids used to a routine so they don't expect you all the time, that's being kind.

All a man's ways are clean in his own eyes.

Bad parenting = poor social skills or likability = parent hates you more and everyone else concurs.

He got bad in memory's dark tunnel where he played it all out, a low archetype gross and wild.

Man is in a fallen state and it really gets ugly, but through Jesus it can all be corrected quickly.

They weren't hating on you but the demon within, yet it sure feels like that when in deep sin.

Lied to while in a fallen state: that's the device used to keep you in hate.

Don't try to be nice or elegant, just be decent and that covers it.

Do not EVER take advice saying to forgive everything without repentance for they are of Satan.

When you come to a new place put up fence/locked gate. No one can impose/it's just your place.

Psychic opening is Aperture Syndrome: locked in a higher dimension as past dissolves/it's fun.

FRENEMY LIAR

You must now stand up for truth. Stop walking on eggs, bring light to your culture, thru you.

When men are emotional, have doubt/fear/anxiety about life/can't stand up it's all anger blocked up.

The most important thing for you to do is sit/dream and do nothing then wait for God's blessing!

They were able to guilt you like an ingrate cuz you went to their dam party, sealing your fate.

You were the one giving them an inroad. Your home became a leaky boat on the wrong road.

I finally saw it: Rather than having a happy Saturday in bliss I had to put up with your s--t.

Watch out for the spirit of familiarity where the maids subtly divide the couple employing them.

Keep distance. Don't be influenced just cuz he's cutting the hedge--there's reasons for this.

Broken homes, lost youth, substance abuse.

Attacks are amazing when you stand for truth. But despite their hazing speak boldly, do it.

The friend of my enemy is my enemy.

You sit on a pile of brilliant/creative work so now just wait to be discovered and repent you jerk.

FRENEMY LIAR

How to maintain a home: Keep stuff out.

"I enjoy cleaning it because it's so beautiful and she keeps it so neat". KK housekeeper.

Keep house by keeping people out cuz in a minute demons bring down whole lot/paradise blocked.

The children of alcoholics have the devil in themselves, that's how Systems Theory works.

Nothing is too beautiful. Nothing is too expensive. Ettore Bugatti

Repent/self-forgive when Satan had the upper hand in your personality and your mind was a sieve.

When you saw it was wrong in that very minute you got over it and God does not remember it.

To God the past doesn't exist (He's in this moment) so just move forward, you were unaware.

Love **your home, see it as your Throne. Choose who comes in but the very best is being alone.**

It's contact = conquest. Don't let her back in or the template and distorted implant reconnects.

God doesn't love you as you are, He said to repent.

Never put household in jeopardy by letting in the less than trustworthy. Instead, have victory.

FRENEMY LIAR

The minute you see your own evil and stop blaming people it's over and God forgets it, for real!

I was too weak/boundaryless. I let em all in and decades went by in a haze of meaninglessness.

I too lost my sanity from a spirit within me and it took years to see it/unravel back to first reality.

When I think of the pain she put me thru. Always budding in/coming over when I told her not to.

Real living is climate control or it's a s**thole.

My heart is very big and that's the problem. I take and overlook until I don't then watch out.

I take a vacation then come right back to it as a servant to God and I have so much fun with it.

If they demonize you cuz you don't agree with them that's a spirit, believe it.

Truth is lacking and he who departs from evil makes himself a prey but God knows there's no justice here today.

Forgive only with repentance then cover it, overlook it, never tell anyone about it.

Christianity is a middle eastern religion, yet how many are left?

Don't you wanna know what it was before advising me to forgive? Without repentance, are you kiddin

FRENEMY LIAR

To me, a thinker, resolving contradiction is more important than eating, sleeping or just living.

If I don't resolve contradiction life is sluggish, I'm skittish, can't fixit till I resolve it and then I'm LIT.

No apology for evolving past your comfort zone cuz you're the dumbest person I've ever known.

I do what I do, and it's you judging me not me judging you.

The lady said "I'm never gonna answer the phone again and always wanna be locked in".

I've always wanted various rooms and views. I can no longer track too: just bible, music, verse.

After the big event (you were so jealous of) their lives were mowed down and their glory gone.

Relativism says we are all beautiful--stubby, short, deformed or fat but the truth says we are not.

Greek ideals: Not everyone's beautiful but we can all aspire and dream and that's wonderful.

We are made in the image of God--we can do anything! But sin degrades that: ugly, fat, stink.

After being shattered I finally figured: it'll all be ok if I stay away.

FRENEMY LIAR

Oh, the difference no longer being eclipsed by others I let in when I was weak/let down my guard!

Is being noticed a form of success?

Self-restraint, superior routines and tricks for creativity-inducement all mark the intelligent.

If things aren't sailing then get away, stop, turn on the music, look out the window: now all is ok.

After being so messed up in original pain what took it away was a locked fence and now I'm all ok.

Calvinists don't wait for anybody. Start your bible study on time don't adapt to their laxity.

Success isn't fame/fortune it's *insulation*. What made me free was not money but a fence/protection.

Just look out the window and music is optional. Don't let your mind be tracked by details ya know.

It you've great talent, sex sins will diminish and end it—must conserve your energy to make it.

Talented but simpleminded are swept up into filthy culture producing a lackluster, pointless career.

You're cute now but give it a little while, you'll show the ugly sin effects: look at Johnny Depp.

FRENEMY LIAR

How to work: party first. Leisure is key to genius creative action, it's been proven by the best.

Relax, all the crap you did was due to demons now gone so with this remorse, be done.

You're too explicit fighting sex sin. Have some class, bring beauty back, don't make things worse.

Weekends are right brain: the magic of Saturdays when mind is untracked and can roam unchained.

So as a creative artist I start my weekends on Tuesday or even Monday. Then it's all creativity.

Self-control is a fruit of the spirit and a strength. Without it you're pulled down with no success.

Stop being impatient, your getting better and better every moment so just relax, it's epic.

Don't adapt to them in what you say. Every moment define you're own way-- too compliant, not ok.

If a genius you'll find your greatest success in the right brain not the left, it's all a unique gift.

In a very short time watch them fall though they look great now.

Stop being a leaky boat giving your energy to this or that affection, get in gear, do somethin'

It's what you do. It will turn fun as soon as you focus so stop worrying about this/win the highest.

FRENEMY LIAR

How people control you: by taking up your time and your mind.

Nothing wrong with living your own life though it may mean never answering/leaving/visiting.

The day you get your life back will be the happiest day of your life. No adaptation, no strife.

At first saying "no" brings guilt. But within a very short time you're absolutely thrilled/killed it.

Why graft them in, you were perfect before.

Let nothing track your mind, close every door. It's a psychic opening to eternity and to soar.

It's contact = conquest. That's right, the mere contact makes you the worst after being best.

Stay away, don't go where angels fear to tread. They know nothing but you're at your crest.

I like the crow in the mornings, the crickets at night, the cows walking by but to humans, byebye.

I just made it all available to ya'll and I'm patient but soon you'll see the rare value/it's a mint.

You don't judge on appearances but their works—what are they producing good or cursed?

It's not the end but the beginning of the end and you're at your apex (highest game) my friend.

FRENEMY LIAR

You don't hate anybody, you just wanna do your own thing. But to win the booty means rejecting.

Take control or they'll mow you under. Be strong cuz there's a severe undertow to human nature.

God judges arrogance let alone the evil chasm into which we've fallen--all planned/not by chance.

Stop your evil gestures. They're embarrassing, low class and gross--seek and act much higher.

Pot makes them normal, it holds them together. Then later early abuse comes back, a repeater.

Fallen Hero Syndrome. They admired him so when he fell wanted to kill him: inversions of humans.

Stop saying you're talking to the dead, that's necromancy and it's wrong, deadly, occult, nasty.

Go into solitude and they can't bug you anymore. Here's where they lose control so I recommend more.

Decades were lost due to a demon you got when you met him. Every day clean the slate amen.

Social nature is a mass of cobweb illusions of who said what to whom and I'm done (whew).

All my life no one would let me concentrate. They'd call my name, knock on door/call on horn.

Life is one big soap opera with people constantly finding out they can't trust someone, what fun.

FRENEMY LIAR

Shut up: that's all I can say to past introjects, memories, botherers, interlopers, opinion leaders.

Talk/gossip all you want, witch. I'm with God now enjoying each moment outa your ditch and rich.

When you fall off pedestals it can be devastating. A sudden fall from grace in the human race.

It's not that I don't wanna be with you I just wanna be alone with no one around.

Relax into conflict, have a simple life, be as a child always in prayer and He'll do all the rest.

Let your work stand on it's own--not needing wordy sophistic explanations but well-known.

When conflict comes, relax in it. Don't get high, call or shirk but be still and see God at work.

Be still in the conflict, watch God work: be free, never having to worry about that one again.

Don't drink, endure the pain--instantly God takes over again. Remember this in the dreary rain.

Pray, He watches. Pray, He resolves/nourishes. Pray, you're carried in a stream as He encourages.

They can't help it. People in a fallen state do crazy things cuz Satan is their father: get this.

A gossip betrays a confidence but a trustworthy person keeps a secret. Proverbs 11: 13

FRENEMY LIAR

The intelligent see things as obvious that the other's don't--it's gonna be a problem so stay alone.

For good relations understand that others can't see what you see nor draw conclusions that quickly.

Problem with high IQ is other kids. Learning not to be arrogant you end up a nerd/unpreferred.

Don't confide in an angry person because when they gossip, they tellin' everyone/you're done.

In dense generations the intelligent aren't even nerds, just alien.

Your IQ is the size of the gun, wisdom says where to aim it and education is the ammunition.

Life success: Intelligence, wisdom and education. You need all three to effectively apply them.

You can be the greatest sinner there ever was but still hate it. Hate sin then soon be free of it.

Sorry I was offended by you not being religious--how ridiculous--but now I see you're the best.

Trauma doesn't lower IQ but makes em mis-use their intelligence molded by the wrong premise.

The more traumatized you are the less ability to use your natural intelligence (no knowledge).

It's called the "blessed hope"--we should be looking for the Lord all the time and yet we mope.

FRENEMY LIAR

Getting a fence and a locked gate was the transformation as life went from bad luck to great fate.

If there's hope in you it separates you from the world as you purify yourself and wait for Christ.

I was like a fish swimming upstream, gulping and drowning. A leaky boat with evil spirits bugging me.

Many are social and love constant interruption but I was the opposite, it caused anger and frustration.

I wanted to go deep inside and that meant total solitude and even my pets knew I needed quiet.

Invasion of my privacy (coming over without calling) even hurt physically, inwardly angry.

I was too weak to assert boundaries from a unique need for solitude so progress could ensue.

The weakest thing I did was to let em in. I had every right not to but I really didn't see that then.

It's such a social generation that if you're inward (saint/genius) they'll hate you/smear.

I fell from a penthouse driving a jaguar to original system surrounded by haters filled with derision.

When sensitives don't assert boundaries (let em in) they invert to most social ending in tragedy.

Same addictive process to any poison: needing it more but enjoying it less while losing all vision.

FRENEMY LIAR

People can be cruel until they begin to die then mostly humility no more invincibility or acting silly.

My office door reads "do not disturb" and "do not knock" but they do both so guess it's too much.

To work I have to be in the right brain and that means NO pressure cuz it's all mental hazard.

I'm jealous of my privacy, what's happening to me? said the queen bee always bugged by thee.

When I'm with em I have to adapt and it bogs me way down so thank you but I'd rather stay home.

We become what we resent. If we hate the mother we become just like her: e.g. angry, indecent.

They just don't want a woman to work cuz she's expected to be focused on the jerks (like a curse).

Whether or not it sells is no barometer so stop asking me that and get real cuz I still have zeal.

To finish all you must do is focus. Nothing to figure out, same simple skills done when highest.

Nothing to figure out--just focus. You've already done it just make it perfect then genius relaxes.

To get the most outa each moment I gotta be alone cuz it's so deep and involved as it spirals down.

FRENEMY LIAR

A neighborhood of self-contained households--not necessary to go door to door telling all.

Supply all his needs, leave him alone. Give him a work space, pray then you are done.

How to work: Learn to release mental hazards like people dropping in--no more of that friend.

If your home is office and you don't have a sec to block em must learn boundaries on your own.

You had the devil in ya and it was horrible, blight on America but Jesus erased it all, remember?

What's wrong with it? It takes hold of ya, you're possessed by it, always thinking of it--the pits.

Two trees outside my window are the tallest/most beautiful I've ever seen, breeze thru leaves.

I bought the house to stay in it always and never have anyone around.

Stop braggin' about how you keep nice home or get things done because trouble may come.

Even asking me a question is a mental hazard from then on.

I do not live in a social reality that other thing was just an emergency.

Just the fact you went thru it means you had to learn it since knowing it you'd never succumb to it.

FRENEMY LIAR

Don't panic over work nor force the fit, it'll do you good to focus part of the day *then* get lit.

A home should run like a Swiss clock not chaos. If people are dropping in that crap must stop.

By loving your home you stay longer on earth.

Two separate nervous systems/brains: active vs. receptive. Tunnel-vision focus vs. wide/diffuse.

The problem with creativity is you can't force it. You develop routines to shake it loose instead.

Focus: Sit at work space, no interruptions, there to do a job, pray--this is empowerment.

No you can't force creativity but you can be smart and provide the space and TIME to focus.

You could be mentally free like a child or entrenched in a human system, a cobweb of illusions, wild.

My family were Calvinists: stoic, tea-totaling, thin, restrained, frugal, devout, routined, happy.

The Lord calls us out of bondage. That's outa the world and it's ways into His kingdom = fantastic!

If one isn't solidly with Christ God they naturally fall into satanic groove which is strange/odd.

What have you to be ashamed of? You love God, they don't--it's sin and sensuality they're made of.

FRENEMY LIAR

You took our kindness for weakness. We feel sorry for you cuz once we start you'll end up passed.

The Spirit of Liberty has risen and I'm telling you it's the season.

To create you need a click in your head and that won't come feeling pressured/forcing the fit.

Relax, true creativity (from God) flows thru when supposed to then you will be through.

The minute I lock that gate I'm in heaven, my own little inner paradise: no interruptions, no more lies.

Knowledge of evil is understanding manipulation and distortion.

Since he's leaving the earth (dying) it's opened me up to new thoughts or what to leave aside.

Parents kill kid's pets without knowledge or permission, just given the information--a lifelong burden

Failure to launch syndrome: Not just not thriving but with parents you're living.

No one can accuse me of being angry if they never see me.

I don't do all the things you're doing. I just move from room to room writing, thinking, viewing.

Work not to give up--it's too easy to get into that slump.

He promised protection and peace and all he needed in return was your silent obedient consent.

Look away, ignore. Don't debate (mean fate) just walk away/close the door.

FRENEMY LIAR

The only reason you keep leaving home is cuz you haven't made it into paradise, never to roam.

No I don't wanna go to a city or a party, and no I don't need any food. Just wanna stay home/cruise.

Just want my own life, reality, viewpoint, things, and SPACE. Life's happy only with a locked GATE.

When you say things that are dark, dirty or mean it congers in my mind so please stop/don't remind.

Don't give in or world goes black. Must be strong enough and mean it: "I don't want you back".

Bad associations bring/keep you down. With the mere contact (conquest) smiles turn to frowns.

Cut it off, nip it in the bud. Cut it off, nip it in the bud. You won't be alone and shoot up to God.

They're like a ton weight holding down a big balloon. You would shoot to the stars: boom!

Worst hell ever: blind inclusion. Biggest joy ever: discernment and exclusion.

It's priceless as the facade dissolves.

I can't work till I have a click in my head so I'll party till then.

It's a vague archetype in their mind then they fill it in (connect the dots) with misinformation.

All this time you thought it's ALL-OK when it's not. You think you're cool but you're rot.

FRENEMY LIAR

It's their constant invitations/requests that control your mind and time, so be inaccessible friend.

Become refined and leave this grossness behind. Hear the crickets, birds, distant bells/so fine.

If I wait for the click in the head it'll all get done but if I force it none so until then have fun.

I learned about life the hard way, a Ph.D. in the streets about how to manage crazy people.

Everything bad I left behind in California but here I'm good cuz I won't open my gate to ya.

Don't give in to this crap all around because they are so off base and their declension is profound.

Yak yak yak, so self-important aren't they.

Just keep em away for one more day I pray.

They love social cuz they lack inner life.

The constant invitations are only interruptions to yours and God's plan so don't give in/refuse em.

After the event you have emptiness. It's addiction: needing it more but enjoying it less.

People die differently. Dad gave up to watch all day TV, mom looked out the window to eternity.

It's all fine and good if you wanna talk like that but I can see right through it.

If we're right we know we're right and don't mind saying it. That's not arrogance it's by studying.

FRENEMY LIAR

Those who believe in God and living it are your real family now, not always by blood.

Cut it all loose in order to just develop on your own accord--that's what you need more of.

All my life I pined for him and now he's gone--what a waste of time/heartthrob.

Don't wanna buncha words I have to read. Just two sentence quips, please.

Like a thread unraveling a sweater to the end, so too the creative act completes itself/what fun.

Don't worry once the creative clicks you'll finish twice as much or complete it all instead.

By waiting for the click in the head you'll get far more done in the end.

I'm waiting for that click in my head. In the meantime, I'll party on and not think of it.

What ever you must do, put farthest from your mind then with leisure suddenly it all realigns.

Art: why waste time describing it, I wanna look at it.

Don't compromise, life's too short for that.

How to succeed fastest: wait as long as you can before starting until you feel you'll burst.

Can you say this: "I don't like you and want you to leave now"?

Hold back from work until it becomes a tidal wave inside, ready to burst forth.

FRENEMY LIAR

It always helps getting away so keep doing it: take off work for the day.

Solution: ignore em.

Engrained in Marxism is envy, so in social generations solitude is the only way to stay free.

Hanging on to the person who is wrong makes you less fit when the right one comes along.

We acclimate to lower people then don't see the evil and become to the good invisible.

Constant invitations: as soon as you go to one potluck they invite you again/can never satisfy em.

You have nothing to fear against atheists promoting evil. See the truth and you're a protected people.

The enemy is the prince of darkness working thru others.

I'm not wasting time but girding up strength/relaxing into receptivity for the next creative surge.

I'm not wasting time I'm readying for the head click to start again and then complete to the end.

Look out the window doing nothing, now you're producing something.

I am waiting for that click in my head. I must have that click before I start. Paul Newman

It's not a waste to take a break, even a real long one--wait to start then it's like a holy spirit streak.

Like crabs in a barrel they wanna keep you trapped, weak and frail so it's time to cut it loose: sail!

Don't dismay cuz in the land of the blind the one-eyed man is king--you're smart so do something.

Pearls before swine: don't waste too much of your time trying to wake em up, draw that line.

It's not that I can't track it's that I refuse to BE tracked cuz nothing's higher than my own map.

Time is the most valuable asset to a successful life so stop wasting it with time-fillers and strife.

Shaking/trembling from recognitions. You don't know why, you don't have to know why, trust em.

Why would your intuition make you shake and tremble like that? Hold on, you're seeing the cad.

Paul said never rely on appearances. Recall wolves in sheep's clothing--trust these verses.

Over and again you saw him as a sheep and over and again he became a wolf and a creep.

Don't read/browse too much cuz it's all about a hunch (inside) so it'd be better to just retrench.

Dear Lord: I don't like it when You leave. I'm only happy when You're here protecting me.

"There's not a spot where God is not" is false/oneist cuz the holy spirit can withdraw in a minute.

FRENEMY LIAR

Resist the narrative that's all around. Hold on to real values learned when you were young.

When you become whole it's fun dealing with attacks from haters cuz you're always the winner.

You're not Christian if quoting scriptures yet supporting everything wrong like Obama the raper.

Our whole problem is fools and fanatics are sure of themselves yet wise are full of doubts.

Your work must stand on its own/not require your three page explanation but that's "art" in the nation.

The fact that they're all so wrong means you being all so right will float to the top overnight.

It's good vs. evil and good will prevail, people! Must know we'll win, so stand high as a steeple.

The wicked do what their father devil tells em to.

Porn started in childhood, with trauma they ran to it--filled gaps biochemically, never outgrew it.

Everything wilts, everything fades cuz God gave it to us temporarily so focus on Him, truly.

Instead of hating them for what they put you thru thank them for the strength it built in you.

Looking back is going back.

FRENEMY LIAR

Courage inspires you, even this *very* jaded generation of today cuz a flicker can turn to a flame.

Reminding people that they're dumb and have no answers is a perilous business. Stefan Molyneux

How can certainty submerge itself into doubt, promiscuity, uncertainty and selfishness?

"Opportunity cost" is a great breakthrough in rational thinking. Pests block the best/you're procrastinating.

Necromancy (talking to dead) is the occult--it can be tempting but as life degrades watch out.

We can't talk to the dead (necromancy) but we can remember what they said/wisdom-get.

Ancestor religions are necromancy. Wish it were true, to talk to dear old dad would be so easy.

Death is sleep until rapture. If we went up to heaven, we'd have to come back down for sure.

Talking to a dead ancestor it is in fact a familiar spirit and you've fallen before you know it.

We can't talk to the dead, they're asleep until the rapture when Christians will meet Him in the air.

Be sure before asking God to make it happen, it may invite predation.

People are known by who they like and admire so if you still love em after finding out you're a liar.

FRENEMY LIAR

Get ready to die. That means to appreciate this day maximally and transcend all ties.

Leave time to sit and think. Just puttering is the most productive time: rising above rinkydink.

Let puttering and thinking be your default setting. Action reversing with diffuse attending.

The joy of retirement is switching from active to receptive mode. Profitable leisure: diffuse attention.

If you can't take it anymore it's time to retire to the right brain which is timeless, perfect, color.

"We're family" when combined with lengthy self-exaltations shows your immaturity and I'm sorry.

Don't addict to social approval cuz it stops you up. What moves you is disapproval, way to the top.

You're famous with low lives so you think this is it but it's a ceiling you've hit/can't go beyond it.

What is most important? Land and a locked gate, no adaptation to anyone or it's bad fate.

These people are freaky so why can't you see it?

Get ready to die. Leave facebook cuz no one cares here. Return to your own situation, nurture it.

Prepare for death tho' it may be decades off. This keeps you from useless tangents/those who scoff.

RED NEW DEAL

Capitalism brought hundreds of millions out of poverty and socialism killed the same amount quickly. AOC just wants to be boss: It's the female power drive and Jezebel spirit not from God. Enjoy rebuking the socialist witch--we must do this or we could lose our republic very quick. Required Holocaust education is the only solution for the stunning ignorance of the Millennial generation. AOC embraces TYRANNY: A horrible bloody-minded system bringing nothing but human misery. Schools are teaching what AOC is spewing: Tho' socialism killed 200 million, that's not their thinking.

RED NEW DEAL

PRIVACY IS A CONSTITUTIONAL RIGHT!

CAPITALISM SAVED MILLIONS COMMUNISM KILLS EM
ARCHETYPE OF EVITA
THE MILLENNIALS WANT FREE STUFF
REFUGEES COMPLY WITH THE BOSSES
UGLY CRUEL FEMINISTS
FALSE PROPHETS GLORY IN ACCEPTANCE
ARROGANCE SELF-DESTRUCTS
TRUE ART DOES NOT POLITICIZE
SWEET SOLITUDE AFTER ALL THIS
THE HOME IS A SACRED SANCTUARY
FORGET THE PREPARATORY STAGE
BE STRONG: SAY NO TO SIN
SIN MAKES LIFE A HORROR MOVIE
FAME IS PROPER COMPORTMENT
A WALL AND LOCKED GATE: GOOD FATE
IT'S A NEW SEASON, A NEW DAY
BE LIKE A FARMER: PLANT THEN WAIT
KEEP GROWING, THEN SUDDENLY...
SUDDENLY: THE ANY MOMENT DOCTRINE
FALL INTO YOUR LAP
DAM THE SOCIAL PECKING ORDER
THE STUPID LOVE SOCIAL
AMERICANA IS INDEPENDENCE & PRIVACY!
SOCIAL HALL RELIGIONS OF ACCOMODATION
I HATED THE SORORITY TOO
IT'S HOLY TO BE ANTI-SOCIAL
GOLDEN RULE SENDS YOU TO HELL
NOT BORN THAT WAY
LATE LIFESTYLE
GET TO SAFETY AWAY FROM THE COASTS
NO ONE UNDERSTANDS HYPERSENSITIVITY
KAREN KELLOCK DISCOVERY IN 84 BOOKS

RED NEW DEAL
PRIVACY IS A CONSTITUTIONAL RIGHT!

How we hate it when creepy arrogant upstarts take over! When everything's reversed, the old COWER!

AOC's calls to abolish ICE endangers her community and the whole country and you love that phony?

AOC'S gratuitous meanness against Reagan: the most beloved president of the last fifty years, forsaken.

AOC talks of pipe dreams but it is REALITY AND TRUTH that 100 million people were killed with socialism.

CAPITALISM SAVED MILLIONS COMMUNISM KILLS EM

Capitalism brought hundreds of millions out of poverty and socialism killed the same amount quickly

AOC just wants to be boss. It's the female power drive and Jezebel spirit not from God.

Enjoy rebuking the socialist witch--we must do this or we could lose our republic very quick.

Required Holocaust education is the only solution for the stunning ignorance of the Millennial generation.

AOC embraces TYRANNY: A horrible bloody-minded system bringing nothing but human misery.

AOC is a tyrant who would dress in $5000 pantsuits flying all over while she puts you in straights, dire.

EEUUWW Saw pictures of spring break: dirty, debauched, arrogant, lost, drunk, so unattractive, yuk!

Schools are teaching what AOC is spewing. Tho' socialism killed 200 million, that's not their thinking.

RED NEW DEAL

Some white men seem cuckholded around AOC and it's sickening but others object without blinking.

How could this stupid communist be taking over like this? Are white men so cuckholded with feminists?

You must enjoy rebuking the socialist witch: do it now or lose the republic quick.

ARCHETYPE OF EVITA

She's playing the archetype of Evita controlling an entire nation. Playing it out, killing us in the process.

AOC Style: Stupid stated with authority but it's almost like a psyop masterminded elsewhere.

Lord relieves the fatherless and widow but the way of the wicked He turns upside down. Psalms 146: 9

Rescue and deliver me from the hand of foreigners. Psalms 144: 11

They have so much to learn but the trouble is they don't know it yet so if you hang on, you'll be burned.

When you care more for foreigners than your own that's TREASON--for decades that's how it's been.

Border deniers call emergency/need for military as "fear mongering" cuz they can't face the conquering.

Woefully ignorant liberals actually compare the holocaust (where millions died) to Islamaphobia: LIES!

Stupid Millennials actually conflate the holocaust to Japanese internment or even LBGT persecution!

The are so used to not-judging they judge nothing and that is hell for our country, believe me.

RED NEW DEAL

To AOC: Americans pursue upward mobility through *hard work and opportunity* knowing nothing's for free.

Capitalism, also known as Free Enterprise, is based on FREEDOM to live your own life/make a good living.

AOC: The claim that freedom and liberty should give way to government control and dictatorship is tyranny!

History is replete with dead or dying nations who have succumbed to socialist politicians like that witch.

THE MILLENNIALS WANT FREE STUFF

The Millennials love AOC cuz they just want free stuff/not to have to work and they don't know anything.

They want personal dictatorial power as The Boss and of the welfare of all of us they couldn't care less.

Venezuela should be the siren sound warning against those tempted by this socialist so renowned.

Democrats are now controlled by socialists and anti-Semites and so will lose the presidency in 2020.

There's nothing more socialist than a "list". When Stalin did it millions were killed but ok if AOC is pissed?

With LISTS first people lose their privileges then more and more is lost until finally they're killed, get it?

The real problem with Cortez is she embraces TYRANNY: making "lists" is the end of you and me.

If you're not towing the party line you go on a list and first it's just privileges then burning whole villages.

LISTS: First you lose privileges, then your rights, then your life. Cortez is the worst in this socialist fight.

RED NEW DEAL

I congratulate those taking on these justice creeps. When we must defend common sense it reeks.

As the RADS take over the democrats we know we have 2020 in the bag cuz they are so ridiculous.

Now they've turned the aggressor into the victim--what liberals always do while we just wanna get on.

Capitalism brought hundreds of millions out of poverty and socialism killed the same amount quickly.

It used to be never trust anyone over 30, now it's don't trust anyone over 30 grand. Dennis Miller

Do we really have free speech today if millions feel **TERRIFIED** of speaking their minds? In no way.

REFUGEES COMPLY WITH THE BOSSES

If citizens aren't in political process they'll be flooded with refugees who will comply with the bosses.

Like Jusse Smollett they **SEEK OUT** victimization-adulation and if they don't get it you're the causation.

Anyone voicing opposing opinions is oppressor and all speech disagreeing with victimhood is hate speech?

They threw paper airplanes cuz I wouldn't say "he and she" rather than "he". I imploded at em honey.

There is no man so smart, so wise and so great as to be able to determine the destiny of his neighbor.

The dam virtue signaling women are leftists are don't even know it. They bought the lie the dumb twits.

Globalists want us homo since that's depopulation. They want us perverted to kill the family and nation.

RED NEW DEAL

I've finally left the news tho' I'll never give up the fight. I've done my part and now will enjoy no-strife.

Manly feminists threw paper airplanes cuz I wouldn't say "he and she" so I happily left the university.

UGLY CRUEL FEMINISTS

Ugly cruel female students were the meanest. I refused to conform to their pronouns, they insisted.

This breakdown was happening in the 70's so I can imagine how bad colleges are now, such a tragedy.

Those with most energy become the worst of the lot when conforming to the debaucheries of the mob.

They just took it for granted that's how you're supposed to act--like an ass--conforming to the mass.

Why couldn't congress pass the BORN-ALIVE bill? Cuz they're evil, wretched and callous as hell.

How could you not hate feminists they are infanticists!

You're a DEMOCRAT? You mean you're for murdering live babies after birth--why you stupid dirty rat!

OMAR: YUK! Calling our great president "not human". Along with AOC these two insurgents are vermin!

It's a much bigger deal than you know letting dumb socialist females rule--puppets for mass murder, "cool".

The stupid Millennials want free stuff/not to have to work. That's the sole reason they love these jerks.

Globalist Gameplan: 1. Take Civics out of the schools, induce America-hate. 2. flashy socialist puppets: instate.

GOSPEL OF ACCOMODATION

RED NEW DEAL

"Gospel of accommodation" adapts to the weaknesses and desires of sinful men, it's false or watered down.

The gospel of accommodation adjusts the gospel to appease/attract sinners and it's all-ok with liberals.

The cum-bah-ya gospel is just an American cultural invention usurping the evil sides of riches and sin.

It appeals to white prosperous America and was invented out of hell itself never mentioning sin or repentance.

False gospel is taking over all churches, many mega. It's "seeker friendly" delivered in short skits to grab ya.

Seeker friendly: You don't like suits or choirs, we'll do away with them. Tell us what you want, friends.

Through computers they design programs making it comfortable for sinners-- no repentance, just be winners.

The gospel of another Jesus sounds sweet but it is not the gospel that I preach. words of Paul 2 Cor 11:14

The gospel of another Jesus sounds sweet but it is not the gospel that I preach. 2 Cor 11:14 by Paul

They're gonna accommodate the sinners, all of their pleasures and needs and make billions with speed.

FALSE PROPHETS GLORY IN ACCEPTANCE

False prophets glory in their acceptance by the world. They deny the law but look so pious it seems ok.

Gentle sheep: sincere, intelligent, bright--but inside they are raving wolves who dampen your joy tonight.

Raving wolves are starved for recognition and gratification, judging success by how big the churches are.

RED NEW DEAL

Can a man of God start right only to become a devil in the pulpit, a minister of Satan? Such changes happen.

If the preacher starts seeking numbers and success it'll change the pastor into a devil, his sermons a menace.

The religion of accommodation is entirely boring to a true Christian--not just cum-bah-ya but sickening.

It's strange that they hate you for doing good but no good deed goes unpunished, understood?

ARROGANCE SELF-DESTRUCTS

Arrogance looks that way--you wanna kill it. But it also falls quickly, mowed down--God took care of it.

Not only a poor housekeeper but what she's into like "The View". Spouting her opinions imposed by shrews.

Yuk three times you lazy witch. You're above housework cuz you're a liberal and loving but just a leech.

They see women as perpetual victims and little innocent darlings but they're the worst to their own honey.

It's the chic fashion to vindictively shaft men. There's a billion dollar industry for divorce and abuse even.

Anti-male bias is so entrenched in law enforcement and courts men don't stand a chance, just the hearse.

"Artists" jump on the bandwagon confirming how bad men are in their works leaving us angry or bored.

The New Rads in congress blame being shunned on racism when it's just their bloody ugly poor character.

TRUE ART DOES NOT POLITICIZE

RED NEW DEAL

Silly works of "modern art" are so stupid, wretched and far-fetched they're not of God but the witches.

New Rads are so embarrassingly presumptuous the way they approach congress in pure arrogance!

I was an embarrassingly arrogant presumptuous female too--all from a false view learned in schools.

They think the POWER they crave comes from acting that way rather than building character which pays.

There are NO social justice artists. For True Art opens the mind to expand and reflect God, the *mostest*.

True Art does not politicize or fall on trendy topics to get the approval of dimwits so please get beyond this.

Just as POCs take over more refined gentile whites, creepy upstarts in congress intimidate the old guys. SAD

SWEET SOLITUDE AFTER ALL THIS

I'm not saying I'm better than you but it's better for me if alone cuz that's the company I prefer to know.

You take me on my errands cuz I can't drive--and stop and talk, gossip, visit, chatter and waste MY time!

If I'm not ready to write or complete something stop bugging me cuz I gotta have that "CLICK": it's God.

As a sagacious senior I gotta put my foot down cuz you youngins know NOTHING, just clowns.

And you're rude too. Your blatant AGEISM is ever as bad as racism if not worse and you're arrogant fools.

You have NO character, the most important thing. I give you something then you ask for more, greedily.

RED NEW DEAL

A sagacious senior will be run right over unless she puts her foot down against clutter, clamor, whores.

I swear to you if you tell the truth they'll line up to your booth cuz they're hungry for you, the sagacious few.

Things have degraded so much for these are the great-grandchildren of the hippies starting the misery.

Women started saying "F--k housework" in the sixties and each generation gets worse in feminist misery.

If detailed instructions in housework aren't passed down a beautiful orderly homelife is forever gone.

THE HOME IS A SACRED SANCTUARY

The home is sacred, a sanctuary of the self under God, protection from the outer world of dirty secularity.

A loved home is a magic home--attracting what it IS. Little lovely nooks and crannies all carefully fits.

But that magic synchronicity of a loved home is missing with irregularity, lack of routine, lazy slovenliness.

He that has gets. Old saying

You've finished your work, a masterpiece. You must rest before rule then new life is joy without ceasing.

No worries--you will come to their mind at just the right time.

Most importantly about your work: Let it sit. Don't finish right away, let it percolate--leave a space!

Being invaded by idiots was such punishment I never got over it.

I gotta wait for that click in the head. NEVER, EVER start before then for it's Holy Spirit Ease instead.

RED NEW DEAL

What is the greatest lesson given by a first class artist? WAIT, WAIT for that click in the head to assist.

Must have total faith in the head-click to begin. Just party, dream, write and plan before then.

It's a New Day, just forget everything yesterday

We're the only ones with free will. The angels cannot deviate and the animals rule totally by instinct.

There's two stages: preparatory & success. In the first stage I learned that life can be bad, a real mess.

In my early life I learned to have boundaries or they'd run over me. And to avoid the bad or life was a tragedy.

FORGET THE PREPARATORY STAGE

Forget everything from preparatory stage cuz it was embarrassing, humiliating and dangerous, sage!

In the prep stage you were low, weak inhabited by evil spirits--compelled to rear it and become a nuisance.

It was all part of your training but now these memories hold you down, failing-- forget to start climbing.

If I think back to the lower stage I get anxious, angry, resentful and tragic cuz it's so low compared to now.

If I ruminate over past failures the brain reads it as instructions and I'll fail again: RELEASE that energy, man!

The user creeps in the past were just TRAINERS cuz before then you had no experience with deceivers.

God's perfect will is like a groove. When addicted you're outa grace--a disgrace--and can't move.

RED NEW DEAL

Your early stage we'll call "primitive" and who you are now "evolved". That oughta explain a lot.

Stop thinking about past creeps, users, abusers, confusers or invaders or all your defenses re-emerge.

The insanity of the past must be regarded as "just a lower level" when your weakness attracted devils.

It wasn't you! Don't you know that when WEAK demons can take over while people blame you, brother?

BE STRONG: SAY NO TO SIN

Be strong: Say NO to sin. That starves it out so the compulsion is gone. Give in = now you're back in.

At a certain point God will bring you out. After all you're doing HIS job and the Potter is done with the pot.

Resistance builds muscle so thank enemies who made you hustle when nothing else could assist at all.

Naturally those with more energy reflect the sick culture in weirdest and most extreme ways: a horror!

I always saw it as a herd cuz I was always the odd girl out--always alone and couldn't stand the mob.

That's what makes social psychology so fascinating: it truly is a herd--mass hysteria and the absurd.

Why would they be jealous of someone who worked every day of their long life on something? Herdlings

The herd flows together: it moves right, it moves left, it's directed from on high and I said goodbye.

I'm sick of following it too: it's too exhausting and frustrating hearing about the arrogant, ignorant and cruel.

RED NEW DEAL

The End of my 84th book on The Herd. Once it's done I'm also done cuz I want to go inside to the Lord.

The herd is like a flock of birds: Flying in perfect unison no one questions the flight pattern itself.

I don't fit, I don't like kissing and hugging in social situations and I'm bored-- nothings as good as alone.

It's also a strain cuz I can read their minds. It's mental confusion, a cobweb of illusions/misinterpretations.

No intellectual can exist in a situation where must watch everything he says losing all his/her class/sass.

SIN MAKES LIFE A HORROR MOVIE

Life was a horror movie when on the lower level of sins and their consequences but now it's happiness.

Life was a horror on the lower level of sick systems and the interlocking messes but now it's independence.

Must know the past horrors were from what you're now free of: we choose bad or good (heaven above).

Must know repentance wiped it all out: slate's clean and you're pure again by the miracle of Jesus: Friend.

Must know you'll never be down there again unless willingly resuming awful sins with dire results like ruin.

They think God's not looking or He doesn't even exist so they sin only to fall flat into awful consequence.

This biggest realization can kill you or save your life: NO ONE CARES, so start anew by cutting ties.

Absolutely *nothing* happening is a sure sign it's *about* ready to burst open to everything happening.

RED NEW DEAL

The more nothing's happening the more everything's about to happen--that's how nature's always cyclin'.

When you're finally down to nothing/no friends, God shows up--that's what He's waiting for: fill my cup.

What is fame: the proper comportment to never be imposed on again as you stay above bad weather.

When everyone rejects you it's a sign God is moving in to do his miraculous work unencumbered.

FAME IS PROPER COMPORTMENT

What is fame: the proper comportment to never be imposed on again so you can do your thing unfettered.

The genius saints cannot tolerate interruption/imposition whatsoever. They rule the day not the fray.

I can't stand anyone controlling moments. Each is a divine design and I need independence to focus.

Cerebrotonia is fear of disorder: a passionate desire for privacy & solitude without which i'm madder.

One famous discoverer finally said "I've been hit on the head/had a stroke and cannot talk again."

Don't blame them for the imposition you weren't famous enough to stay the hell away from everyone.

It took lifetime to learn the most important word was "NO!" The world wants to rob your destiny ya know.

They wanna take you outa your home, away from your work, while blocking what you think and speak.

They don't want you happily creating or puttering in your own cozy abode. They want you miserable dude.

RED NEW DEAL

Don't blame yourself sweetie you weren't famous enough to say stay the hell away.

We let them in--that's where the trouble starts, hon. They're demons so your "NO" blocks a homewreckin'

I let them in and probably enjoyed their company at first. But I learned the lesson fast about evil jerks.

I let them in--I was a weak woman captivated in my own home by wicked men who were not my friends.

They ruined my life and my home. I know about invasion, loss of privacy and lost freedom to bums.

A WALL AND LOCKED GATE: GOOD FATE

Now the most important thing is a wall and a locked gate with land as a buffer zone--that's a real home.

The more orderly you are the the higher your boundaries the more you feel DISGUST for barbarities.

These are horrible people, hear me? And the youth don't care, are careless, hedonistic, narcissistic, LOST.

Nothing is worse than losing your freedom and having to adapt to other people. NOTHING, hear this!

Stop resenting your guests cuz you let in the pests. See the matrix: it's you who is ridiculously amiss.

Wicked men captivating weak women in their homes: When that knock comes assert you wanna be alone.

YOU'RE the problem: putting the onus where the responsibility lies gives you back your very life.

You woulda been fine alone but when they imposed your whole destiny was blown. Be firm, say "NO!"

RED NEW DEAL

Our present troubles are temporary but resulting glories last forever: boundaries learned from pressure.

The struggle (lesson) is temporary, the blessing is forever.

The most important lesson in life is "NO!". The world wants you to get off your magic track you know.

IT'S A NEW SEASON, A NEW DAY

It's a new season, a new day. My season of tears and overcoming are over and success is on the way.

They've been trained to be horrible people and care-less idiots. Tho' not their fault I still want rid of em.

Reject these losers/abusers and go onto your New Season. Otherwise, you stay in bondage/no movement.

The nice virtue-signaling Baptist lady created pre-convicts by her refusal to discipline the twits.

It wasn't me it was a projection of an introjection: mimicking mom I had swallowed whole, son.

Early trauma stops development then to adapt to it we introject (swallow) others then repeat their script.

Hurray, today's your day! For your time has come after a long preparatory history covered by Thee.

Thank all your interlopers for teaching you the importance of boundaries and managing crazy guys.

God made me forget all my hardships and prospered me double. Joseph in names of his sons

Seasons are unforced rhythms of nature. Get that word: UNFORCED, you can do nothing but wait sir.

RED NEW DEAL

The Lord preserves all who love Him but all the wicked He will destroy. Psalms 145: 20

Nothing is wrong, it's not the right time. Wait for your season: work, then relax knowing it'll happen.

Success Plan: It's not all harvesting: there are seasons of watering, planting, pulling up weeds (pruning).

Are we gonna keep a good attitude when we're not seeing growth or making progress? God notices this!

When you stay in peace knowing God's in control, you're like a tree bringing fruit in it's season, that's all.

BE LIKE A FARMER: PLANT THEN WAIT

Farmer who does all that KNOWS there will be a harvest so just relax and plan for when you're a starlet.

Bible implies there will be waiting periods when we see NO GROWTH. It's part of the process, KNOW it.

You're STUCK. There's nothing wrong it's just timing, you're in that waiting period preceding good luck.

When you come into your season you'll bear much fruit but the question is how you act before your reboot?

There is NO struggle coming into your season: you just naturally bear much fruit cuz that's God's attribute!

BECAUSE you did the right thing when it was slow God'll bring you into harvest season and the dough!

Timing: If God promoted you before you were ready it wouldn't be a blessing but a burden, believe me.

The Season of Waiting is all part of it. God uses this season to do a work in you so be THRILLED by it!

RED NEW DEAL

If you have faith and patience in this waiting period your faith and character grows to be **READY** for it.

Giving a kid a car at ten isn't a blessing but a curse. It's the same thing with us so **WAIT** for God's perks.

If God would've given you what you wanted it would have limited your future: He sees ahead for sure.

Trust God's timing: "NO" doesn't mean never, it means "not right now". God is omniscient, you know.

A good father has a good gift ready, but he won't give it at the wrong time knowing it would be deadly.

KEEP GROWING, THEN SUDDENLY...

Keep growing, giving and passing the test. God sees the BIG picture so trust and rely on the Best.

The person you'll need may not be ready--the one to be instrumental in your success towards plenty.

Be patient and go through the waiting period with a great attitude and you'll be successful even rich dude.

Not yet, be patient, you're in a waiting period but your SEASON is coming--your ship's prepping to come in.

The steps of a GOOD person are ordered by the Lord. The steps of a sinner are empty, wrong and soured.

Joseph kept passing the test in waiting periods: When it was unfair, when betrayed or robbed.

Without patience you'll get stuck. Without going through the waiting period with a good attitude--good luck!

Joseph knew he must WAIT for God's purpose to unfold. Waiting is the most essential test for gold.

RED NEW DEAL

Joseph was thrown into a pit by his family, imprisoned for what he didn't do. Still he waited cuz he KNEW.

Your Time Has Come when God vindicates you, promotes you and takes you to a brand new level: whew!

When your time has come it's SUDDENLY, immediately: all at once the prison doors are open, oh my!

God comes unexpectedly: out of the ordinary, you didn't see it coming but POW: IT'S HERE, so happy!

All I was doing was the right thing, trudging through the difficulty with faith and hope then God said "HELLO"!

SUDDENLY: THE ANY MOMENT DOCTRINE

SUDDENLY I came into my season, suddenly the whole thing took off, suddenly all enemies were gone.

Suddenly our health improved. One touch of God's favor catapulted me to life dreams in great magnitude!

Just keep thinking how ONE TOUCH of God's favor can catapult you to new levels you never conjured.

The key while waiting is EXPECTANCY any moment your dreams will show up. Remember: ANY MOMENT.

One little break, one phone call, meeting one person and boom: you'll come out of the waiting period, soon.

It's a SEASON of preparation and overcoming, and a SEASON of blessing and influencing while loving.

There are seasons of TESTING and proving then wonderful seasons of promotion and blessing.

God is precise, specific and detailed to the split second. His ways are higher than ours so just trust it.

RED NEW DEAL

A season of abundance and new growth is when God *THRUSTS* you to the new level--are you available?

God is not only ordering your steps but people you'll need. He'll cause em to cross your path, decreed.

Opportunity will find you, good breaks will track you down. You'll meet em in the elevator or in town.

It's been a long time but stay encouraged: God has a SUDDENLY lined up for you and it's so cool!

FALL INTO YOUR LAP

The business will fall into your lap, the problem turned around. SUDDENLY it happens, your mind blown!

My steps are ordered, any moment I'm coming into my season. I love the Lord and that's one reason.

I'm so excited, I'm gonna get my miracle! For surety think back to all the times He made things bearable.

Behind the scenes God is moving the wrong people outa the way, pushing back the forces of darkness, ok?

He's not just bringing you what you want but pushing back the devil's obstructions of lack.

It's your MIND which will attract it in. But you're always thinking of the crazy past--your greatest sin.

They wanna force their vision of utopia on us at gunpoint.

RUDE: Good manners and etiquette demand you never ask a woman's age, salary, weight or carat diamond.

The password to God's bounty is gratitude and praise--a "sacrifice" of praise cuz it's hard in hard times.

RED NEW DEAL

Thank God for everything--key to his heart. I thank You for the invaders who taught me boundaries.

People expect you to adapt to them--it's what I hate and refuse to even try (why should I) so I lock my gate.

Don't even talk to them. They ask rude, personal questions and aren't worth your time or attention.

They size you up and wanna put you down. I've matured beyond society/just want my own reality and home.

DAM THE SOCIAL PECKING ORDER

I don't play that game of the social pecking order. I wouldn't go through that ringer ever, it is disorder.

If they like my books fine if they don't fine. It's God's decision cuz He puts one down/the other up: mine.

I thank You for the rude, impertinent and dangerous dudes who taught me boundaries/need for solitude.

I thank You for the Jezebels I've known for they taught me boundaries also and to just wanna be alone.

God was in these people lessons. Apparently I was so needy for love I sought their bloody appreciation.

Now I see this generation as incredibly dumbed down, few understand what's going on so just be alone.

You don't have to throw em out just learn how to manage em.

The reason women don't like being asked their age: In an ageist society you are JUDGED by your age.

I believe I was sent by God to a social generation that puts conformity to social ABOVE independence.

RED NEW DEAL

It's no sin to want privacy but they act like it is. It's a constitutional right but communists are pissed.

My first housekeeper brought 8 kids with her running all over the house. Never again, I learned my lesson.

People used to big families have no idea about the privacy-essentiality. We introverts are united about it.

People mean adaptation--change. Privacy means no-adaptation--freedom to be yourself even deranged.

Since the sixties the SOCIAL was more important than independence. This is ANTI-American you dunces.

The idea you can't be a scientist unless social is ridiculous. But this was the sway since the 60's: frivolous.

THE STUPID LOVE SOCIAL

The reason you love social is because you're stupid. The deep can't stand it so they are the secluded.

Having minimal friends is adaptive. It leaves space for yourself, the brilliant genius saint so attractive!

They pushed me to be social like nothing else mattered: like brains, creativity and drive--bashed & battered.

My old cat needs her own room or else she's hissing all the time. I understand that because she's mine.

In the Old West they kept pushing out. New neighbors meant moving if within ten miles of em no doubt.

Solitude means going deep inside where the gems are. People means staying on the surface: boring, war.

The Old West was the essence of privacy. You show up on my ranch I appear with a shotgun for liberty!

RED NEW DEAL

Communism: You come home from work finding people in all the rooms--gov says you have enough too.

I don't have a right to my big house filled with artistic design just for me. That's horrible and selfish you see.

Every time she asks me if to rent a room I get nervous. Like I don't have a right to solitude but I resist this.

I was happy deep inside seeking God and self without relatives but society bashed me for lack of friends.

AMERICANA IS INDEPENDENCE & PRIVACY!

What I discovered for people like myself--true Americans--is that most people as just an encumbrance.

Social generations are taught that godliness is social and social is godly. This opposes the truth, surely.

Entering a convent for privacy won't work either. Make your home a sanctuary and love it brother.

I would say nothing is more Americana than privacy and a perfect set up for communism is conformity.

You don't have a right to your comfortable society or homelife. You gotta let em all in despite strife.

The fallen church sees solitude as a sin. Loving God means being social and putting up with sinful kin.

Insisting I be social is putting me into slavery. You don't see this cuz the schools teach idiocracy.

Go ask the farmer down the street if he could house a bunch of people. He's got room for this evil.

The COMMUNE was setting us up for communism. People everywhere is the worst possible prison.

RED NEW DEAL

Because I love privacy they called me mean, selfish, self-involved, haughty, conceited and unloved.

Ask the lone ranger if a bunch of people can tag along. See where that gets you with a true American.

All my life I was imposed on by other people. Well finally I have achieved privacy--high as a steeple!

But still I must FIGHT for it as if I don't have a right to be alone. If I wanted a big family I'd have it, clones!

As a child I was imposed on by drunks then older sisters then society took over but I survived being a pushover.

In this era we're supposed to worship people before God. In fact that's the litmus test: pure facade.

SOCIAL HALL RELIGIONS OF ACCOMODATION

Imagine going to a church seeking God and all you confront is social BS and expectations by the flawed.

In the fallen church the God-seeker gets a brick to carry not a lamp to guide-- no wonder he gave up and died.

NO I don't wanna go to your boring pot lucks. I just wanna seek God in my den for unspeakable joy deluxe.

Don't call it a church but a social hall religion. I will never darken your doors again you den of demons!

I'm Scotch to the core. They had molts around their castles to ensure privacy which they adored.

Church ladies came there chastising me for not being social--that was being "mean" to the people.

In the true church you hear about hell vs heaven on Sundays then enjoy solitude with God the other days.

RED NEW DEAL

They love him cuz he's rich and famous having won acceptance but does he talk about repentance?

To take an innocent child and throw him into the social ringer is cruelty. Few can insist on True Reality.

The biggest achievement in life is the strength to insist on the constitutional right to privacy, to RESIST.

They call me controlling but I don't care what you do. It's just my own home and reality with people FEW.

In communism you come home to people in all your rooms cuz gov decided you were to be doomed.

In prisons it isn't solitary confinement that's torture it's crowded conditions and that's the point, amen.

I HATED THE SORORITY TOO

In college I joined sorority and hated it immensely. All those birds controlling me in a collective female pigsty.

I have a constitutional right to privacy: an achievement after overcoming the social culture of lunacy.

A bunch of dullards smirking and faking it. That's the modern church potluck and I've had enough of it.

We Calvinists are sober, somber and serious. We aren't jocularly jesting like a Cheshire cat, delirious.

In prisons it isn't solitary confinement that's torture it's crowded conditions like the crazy social culture.

Gee Karen you aren't nice! You hate people like they're filled with lice! GTH you bother me--I'll say it twice.

Gratitude's the key to God's bounty. Thank you God for thugs teaching me it's better to be lonely.

RED NEW DEAL

I'm not a hater I'm like the old west ranchers appearing at the door with a shotgun against ambushers.

I love the show DALLAS cuz every other word is "none of your business" even in the family and I love this.

In my Father's house there are many mansions and I'm all alone in them--here there is no more invasion.

We were so happy on our lone hill until you invaded us with your dam social BS until I said "good riddance!"

My poor mother felt invaded/hated it when my friends came around--I never understood why until now.

IT'S HOLY TO BE ANTI-SOCIAL

It is HOLY to be anti-social. Start a new life NOW by putting that on your wall.

In social eras who rules? The devil's crowd.   Cackling laughter like cinders in a fire: alone you're better off.

The stupidest, phoniest and most boring show on TV (loved by youth) was called "FRIENDS".

Introverts have just as much right to exist as extrovert social perverts. Stop telling me to smile jerks.

The way to heaven is not through creeds or social hall religions but through a person: Jesus is the reason.

I was lost goin' to hell without God: no hope like driftwood on a restless sea-- that was me, then He called me.

I was lost with no purpose but He took me from darkness to the marvelous light: He saved me/gave me LIFE!

Don't get discouraged. Your steps are ordered, you're right on schedule--delays precede being nourished.

RED NEW DEAL

From interruption-to-interruption: that's the way life is letting people rule it--waste and destruction.

The reason people never reach their highest potential is cuz they never get away from the wrong people.

Connect with people who understand your destiny and appreciate your uniqueness MORE not less.

False friends never give you their approval no matter how good you do, like crabs in a barrel too.

Life is too short to drag people along. Get them out and God'll bring the right people in: a new song!

GOLDEN RULE SENDS YOU TO HELL

The devil has told people that if they live by the Golden Rule they'll go to heaven--UNTRUE!

Be not conformed to this world but be transformed by the renewal of your MIND. Love God then rewind.

Stop mimicking the devil's thoughts and study God's thoughts which instantly roots that ol' devil out.

The True Americana spirit is independence and privacy--but you could never understand that Missy.

How Satan works: First he suggests something and that suggestion takes root in your mind as a curse.

One wrong thought can send your soul to hell and hold you in sickness all your life as LIES create strife.

Because I was so hurt by them I hung on to "them" then I hung on to "it": the addictive is repetitive.

It was sickening and terrifying having to adapt to lower people: years of learning how to adapt/sequester.

RED NEW DEAL

They accept their demon-induced plight then get mad at God (the marvel) so let's expose this devil.

"I was born that way" is a lie from hell! You were never born homosexual or lesbian--demon spells.

We become entirely different people when we adapt, re-adapt, fall back, create, reinvigorate: good/bad fate.

You were never "born that way" that's a demon power that can be broken and driven out of your life.

The real you is normal and there's an unclean entity (personality) you hate so suicide you contemplate.

You can't keep birds from flying overhead but you sure can keep em from nesting in your hair. John Osteen

The thoughts that disturb you are not your own, they're from an external source--the devil, el stinko.

We know we're with God and power of the world lies with wicked one--but God knows what's going on.

I was blinded by denominational tradition--the devil used that to blind me but God yanked me free.

He knows about my feelings I'm about to die--that is the devil who loves death, disappointment, lies.

God was with me in all my humiliations, rejections and failures. But now I know this curse is all reversed.

Why were they rewarded? Because they repented, turned back to God as they turned from false gods/idols.

His dad is an oldstyle preacher but he's a motivational speaker: key is: heaven/hell/sin/repentance.

God doesn't "talk" to you. Satan talks, God REVEALS. It's a knowing that comes over peoples.

RED NEW DEAL

The fallen church has blinded us to the fact of a hell to shun and a heaven to gain--that we must refrain.

It's not the quantity of friends but the quality. I'd rather have two that are for me 100% than many for less.

LATE LIFESTYLE

Why do people lose their looks with age? FOOD, too much, wrong kind, used as crutch plus drugs/drinking.

Recent studies show that "acid reflux" pains are instead just REACTIONS to chemicals of all kinds.

That pain in the chest/esophagus: that's my first reaction to chemicals and food is the biggest rascal.

Reactions to chemicals feels like carsickness: greyness, biliousness, dizziness, nausea and eventual coma.

Cars are the worst--the most toxic things on the planet, like climbing into a gas chamber but few see it.

Finding a car I can ride in is near impossible. I won't ever go again so don't ask cuz it makes me miserable.

Tho' I'm not a sister wife I adapt to my environment somewhat: rayon tunics, asymmetrical hem, 3/4 sleeves.

I'm not FLDS but neighbors are sister wives in their prairie dresses--it's where I've escaped to happiness.

My neighbors are self-contained units, I hardly ever see em. They mind their own business, God love em!

GET TO SAFETY AWAY FROM THE COASTS

The safest place in America is also the most beautiful. Red mountains wherever I look, houses are red too.

RED NEW DEAL

That way you fit new International modesty style but are still doing your own thing totally and comfortably.

Get em in all colors with matching hats, now you're set. Black unders: now you will look your best.

I recommend everything in Smartwool for winter and Korean cotton for summer and avoid all synthetics.

Got the idea from Joyce Meyer. Asymmetrical hems for modesty, ultra-comfy, wear shorts or pants under.

Hillary coughs uncontrollably/unexpectedly cuz she can't give up the herb--she just loves the superb.

It was hard for me to give up the herb too. But in order to talk I had to quit the cough which was so uncool.

I would call it orthorexic: When I was vegan dieting was an obsession and I spent a fortune/NO FUN.

I refuse to diet now: NO low-carb, keto, carnivore, high carb, lowfat, fruitarian but eating what I want.

We have our routines every morning. I do this then I do that so the cat has stuff she can count on.

Few understand chemical sensitivity so put you me the ringer--since they don't have it, I'm the faker.

NO ONE UNDERSTANDS HYPERSENSITIVITY

No one understands what it's like to be sick all the time: food, perfume, plastics, vinyls with glues.

Every time it's another chemical injury and I get more allergic to more things and that is my whole history.

I never leave home, my oasis and sanctuary from chemicals. The joys of being homebound never ceases.

RED NEW DEAL

Learn of MCS then put your foot down! For the herd will resist and even medicine will put it down.

My home is my oasis, I have an air filter in every room. I live in a bubble and I see you all as fools.

MCS is a matter of D.I.P.--Duration, Intensity, Proximity! They don't just take me to the store but all day.

Duration: I can make it to the country store. But you ADD ON a bunch of other stops and I'm sick/bored!

In homes I feel sick--not just chemicals but disorderliness, not-quite-cleanness, could-care-lessness.

I walk into homes and feel pity for the kids and pets let alone the husband. I will call this female disgusting.

Cars are like being in a gas chamber for the sensitive. I will never go in another vehicle unless first tested.

The car can be ok but what if the driver has detergents, soaps, perfumes and shampoos--forget her too.

I could never enjoy vacations, they had to leave me on the farm to witness weird family dramas I abhorred.

Chemically sensitive are easily aggravated with people's flaws cuz everything is magnified as the cause.

I'm through with food-restriction of any kind. I eat once a day--that's how I stay pretty, ageless and refined.

Reduce total load for maximum adaptation. No digestion past morning to adapt to nightly wood burning.

Every morning my dog wants a BIG HUG. What a doll--he lingers there for minutes cuz dogs LOVE.

CATS are carnivores so stop feeding them vegan food. It's dogs & humans who are omnivores you fools.

RED NEW DEAL

KAREN KELLOCK DISCOVERY IN 84 BOOKS

It's a discovery according to Koestler who wrote Act of Creation and Structure of Scientific Revolutions.

I've reached my peak by completion and now face the decline--but I DID it and deserved success is mine.

You gotta believe more than "He is"--for He is a rewarder. He's not out stealing killing and destroying.

You gotta know He's a GOOD GOD and He REWARDS those who seek Him. And I know it's coming.

Don't work until you can do nothing BUT work--the urge will be that great and it will also mean perks.

I'm thrilled as I sit here knowing it's coming and soon! For He's a good God who knows what I've been thru.

Dear all imposers and imposters: Thank you for teaching me the value of solitude you losers.

KAREN KELLOCK BOOKS:

AFFINITY OR MISERY
AGELESS CORNUCOPIA
AMERICA AWAKE!
AMERICA'S DAFT ERA
ARTS OF PALEO FASTING
AUTOPHAGY ON CHEATERS
BACKSTABBING NEUROTICS
BETRAYAL TRAUMA
BOOMERS AND BROKENNESS
BOOT ON NECK
CHAMPION GUIDES
COMMIE NUTHOUSE
COMMIES
COMMUNIST SPIRIT
CONTAGION OF MADNESS
CONTAGIOUS MADNESS
CULTURE CLASH BASHED
DAFT LEFT
DAILY FASTARIAN
DAM RATS
DIVERSITY IS CRUELTY
E-RACE WHITE
THE END OR A BEND?
FEMALE BULLIES AND FEMI-NAZIS
FEMALE CARNALITY
FEMALE DUMB DOWN
FEMINISM AND RUIN 1 & 2
FIX FOR MISFITS
FOOLS & TRAMPS
FREEDOM SPEAKING
FRENEMY ENABLER
FRENEMY LIAR
FRENEMY THIEF
FRENEMY TRAITOR
TRENEMY TYRANT
GENIUS IS HELD DOWN
GLOBALISLAM
GOD USES THE FLAWED
HAZE OF THE LATTER DAYS

KAREN KELLOCK PH.D.

M.S. Political Science, San Diego State. Ph.D. in Psychology, University of California Irvine. Postdoctoral: UCI School of Medicine, Dept. of Psychiatry [NIMH Grants]. Developed the Debris Theory of Disease, a theory of system pathology in 120 books and 22 textbooks for the general public. The theory has a general formula: All disease is obstruction, all recovery is elimination, all success is attraction. The three obstructions are people, habit and food. Remove obstruction and snap to your goals, waiting in the wings.